Searchlight Books™

Saving Animals with Science

Pet Tech

Lisa Idzikowski

Lerner Publications ◆ Minneapolis

For my family

Lerner Publications Company
An imprint of Lerner Publishing Group, Inc.
241 First Avenue North
Minneapolis, MN 55401 USA

For reading levels and more information, look up this title at www.lernerbooks.com.

Main body text set in Adrianna Regular.
Typeface provided by Chank.

Editor: Annie Zheng **Photo Editor:** Annie Zheng
Lerner team: Sue Marquis

Library of Congress Cataloging-in-Publication Data

Names: Idzikowski, Lisa, author.
Title: Pet tech / Lisa Idzikowski.
Other titles: Pet technology
Description: Minneapolis : Lerner Publications, [2024] | Series: Searchlight books - saving animals with science 01 | Includes bibliographical references and index. | Audience: Ages 8–11 | Audience: Grades 4–6 | Summary: "Taking care of a pet is a big responsibility, but it doesn't have to be impossible. From automatic feeders to web cameras, technology can help readers with all the jobs that come with pet care"— Provided by publisher.
Identifiers: LCCN 2023009357 (print) | LCCN 2023009358 (ebook) | ISBN 9798765609132 (library binding) | ISBN 9798765624784 (paperback) | ISBN 9798765617229 (epub)
Subjects: LCSH: Pets—Juvenile literature. | Pet supplies—Juvenile literature. | Pets—Feeding and feeds—Juvenile literature. | Technology—Social aspects—Juvenile literature. | BISAC: JUVENILE NONFICTION / Animals / Animal Welfare
Classification: LCC SF413 .L39 2024 (print) | LCC SF413 (ebook) | DDC 636.088/7—dc23/eng/2023030

LC record available at https://lccn.loc.gov/2023009357
LC ebook record available at https://lccn.loc.gov/2023009358

Manufactured in the United States of America
1-1009622-51591-5/18/2023

Table of Contents

Chapter 1

PETS, PETS, PETS

In 2022, a California woman named Jessica received a surprising phone call from an animal shelter. Jessica was shocked. Her lost cat, Lily, had been found after almost six years! On average, only 2 percent of lost cats reunite with their owners. But people at the shelter scanned

Lily's microchip, a tiny piece of technology carrying her information under her skin. Because of that, they were able to contact Lily's owner.

Technology played a big part in reuniting Lily with her owner. But technology can do other things for pets too.

PEOPLE AT VETS AND ANIMAL SHELTERS IDENTIFY PETS USING MICROCHIP SCANNERS.

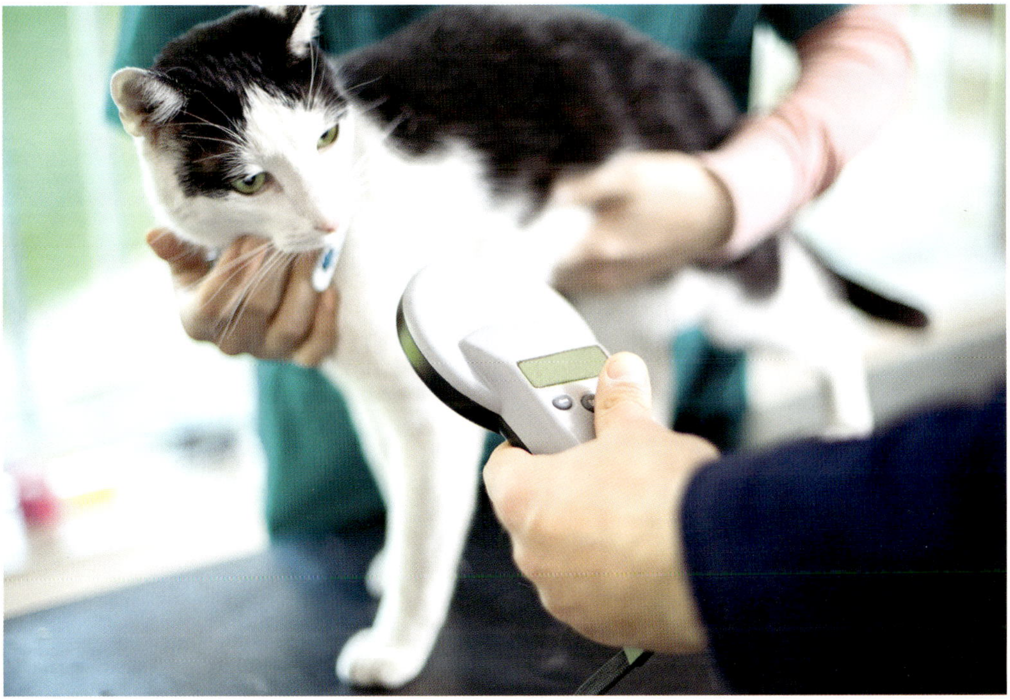

Pet Technology

Pet technology, or pet tech, is technology that helps people take care of their pets. For example, automatic feeding and watering stations provide food and fresh water for pets alone at home. Pet-friendly cameras,

Furbo is a dog camera that lets owners keep an eye on their pets.

A boy loads an automatic tennis ball launcher to play fetch with his dog.

smart toys, and video games help look after and keep four-legged friends entertained when their owners can't be there with them.

And what about safety? Pet tech has produced tracking tools, microchips, automatic doors, and more to keep people's furry pals safe. The possibilities for pet technology are endless.

Chapter 2

EAT, DRINK, PLAY, AND . . . POOP

Pet tech helps make sure pets stay healthy. Discover what technology is keeping them fed, clean, and happy!

Chow Time

According to veterinarians, healthy adult cats should be fed once or twice a day. Dogs should eat at least two meals a day. But what happens if an owner is running late and can't feed them on time? For some owners, an automatic feeder such as a WOpet Automatic Pet Feeder might be the answer.

Unlike other automatic pet feeders, it connects to the internet. Owners with smartphones can download the app to get started. They can use the app to decide when their pet will be fed. They can also say how much food the pet should get. Then the pet feeder will automatically drop the food into the tray at the selected times.

Automatic feeders make planning mealtimes easy.

A cat with the Catit Flower Fountain

Watering Fountains

What if someone forgets to put out a bowl of fresh water? Owners can use automatic watering fountains. The Catit Flower Fountain works for cats and small dogs. It's a round, plastic cylinder that stands 8 inches (20 cm) tall, with a top that looks like a water fountain. An internal filter with thousands of tiny air pockets cleans the water for small pets to drink. The machine can be set to run at a gentle or bubbling stream.

Larger dogs can get clean, running water from the Zeus H2EAU Drinking Fountain. This fountain looks and functions like the Catit Flower Fountain. The top constantly bubbles to keep water moving, so the water won't go bad. Then dogs will always have fresh water to drink.

A small dog drinks from an automatic watering fountain.

Cleanup

Pet tech can help clean up after pets. Most cats use litter boxes, and owners have to clean them at the end of the day. But this might not be a daily chore for long.

Litter-Robot 4 is an automatic-cleaning litter box. Cats walk into the circular opening, do their business, and come back out. Afterward, the robot rotates the litter inside and sweeps the dirty litter into an internal box

Cat coming out of a self-cleaning litter box

below. Cats will have a clean litter box after each time they use Litter-Robot 4. Owners will still have to clean out the box below. But this can be done once a week instead of every day.

Exercise and Play

Dogs need regular exercise to be healthy. Many pet owners play fetch with their dogs to help them be active. But owners can also use pet tech. An automatic tennis ball launcher can throw the ball as many times as a dog wants. A person loads the balls into the machine. Then the balls shoot out. Dogs can get the exercise they need with it. But dogs and their owners aren't the only ones who can benefit from tech toys.

Dogs get exercise from playing with an automatic ball launcher.

A cat tenses up as she waits for the automatic feather to move.

BENTOPAL is a robot that keeps cats entertained and gives them exercise. The machine has a feather and twists and turns so cats can have fun jumping at it. BENTOPAL also has wheels, so cats will have to chase after their toy. This technology keeps cats on their toes.

Some owners might wonder if their pet is getting enough exercise. But they won't have to wonder for long. Just as some people have fitness trackers, pets have them too. Instead of being worn as a watch, these trackers clip to their collars. Owners will have to install an app on their smartphone. But then they can see how much their pet exercises.

FitBark is a fitness tracker that clips to dog collars.

Chapter 3

LOST AND FOUND

Pet owners often attach collars and ID tags to their animals in case they get lost. But what if the collars or tags fall off? Discover what pet tech can do to help keep pets safe!

Microchips

Microchips are small, rice-sized chips that veterinarians place under an animal's skin in case a pet gets lost. Each chip is coded with a unique number that identifies the pet.

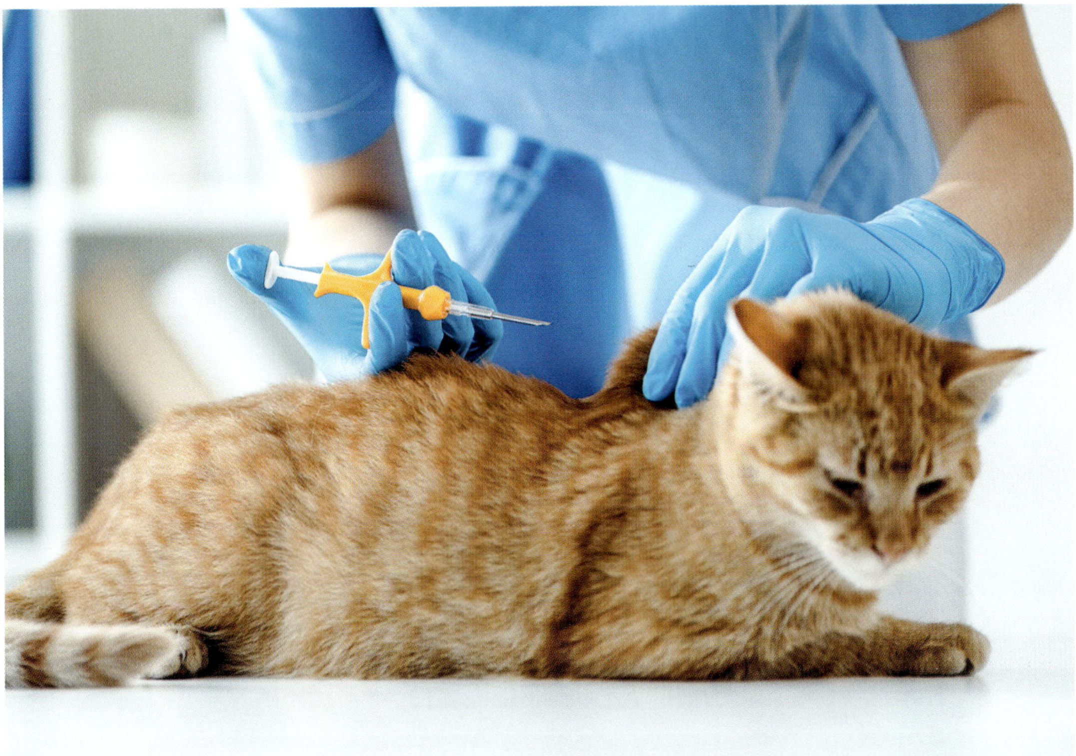

VETERINARIANS IMPLANT MICROCHIPS IN PETS TO HELP IDENTIFY THEM WHEN THEY'RE LOST.

Because each number is different, every chipped pet has a lasting ID. When a lost animal is brought to a vet or shelter, the microchip is scanned. The chip's number helps locate a pet's owner. Cats, dogs, rabbits, horses, birds, and even snakes can get chipped!

Spotlight On

Check the Chip Day

Every two seconds, a pet is lost. That's why the American Veterinary Medical Association and the American Animal Hospital Association introduced Check the Chip Day. Every year on August 15, they spread the word about pet microchip technology. Not all pets get chipped, so these groups encourage pet owners to chip their pets.

The Tile app can help owners find pets at the park.

Track Them

Microchips only work if someone brings the lost pet to a vet or shelter to scan. That's why some pet owners will place a tracker on their pets. Tile is a Bluetooth tracking system. The Tile Sticker model is a small, quarter-sized sticker that owners can place on the animal's collar. The sticker connects to an app. Owners can download the app on their phone. The tracker works up to 250 feet (76 m) away. To locate a pet, click Find in the phone app. Then the tracker will ring so the person can find their pet.

GPS trackers can also help find pets. GPS works by using satellites in the sky to help locate things. These small devices clip onto a pet's collar. They're a bit heavier than the Tile Sticker, but GPS trackers cover a larger area than a Bluetooth system. Whether pets are out on a trail, in a nearby dog park, or around the neighborhood, owners will be able to find their wandering pets.

This yellow GPS tracker lets this dog's owner know where it is.

Deep Dive

The Halo Collar

The Halo Collar is a wireless fence that lets dogs run unsupervised. It uses a collar, a smartphone app, and training. Once owners download Halo's app, they can draw a map of where their dog can and can't go. The app funnels that information into the collar. The collar then uses custom feedback to make sure the dog stays within those boundaries. A beep might mean stop, and a whistle might mean come back.

A dog wearing the Halo Collar

Chapter 4

HOME ALONE

What happens when owners aren't home or can't keep an eye on their pets? Discover how pet tech helps keep pets and their homes safe!

Pet Doors

Some people have had animals, aside from their pets, get inside their homes through pet doors. One woman in Florida even had an alligator crawl through her doggy door, leading her to call wildlife officials.

ALLIGATORS ARE LARGE BUT HAVE BEEN KNOWN TO SQUEEZE THROUGH DOGGY DOORS.

This could have been avoided with smart pet doors.

Smart pet doors recognize individual pets. This technology uses radio-frequency identification (RFID) to recognize pets. It works when an animal has a microchip implanted in its body or is wearing an RFID tag on its collar. The door recognizes the correct signal coming from either the microchip or collar and opens. Only pets that live at that house can go in or out.

RFID tags are small and can easily attach to a dog's collar.

This cat flap reads the microchip inside a pet's body to know to let it in.

Artificial Intelligence

Someday pets might not need a microchip or special collar to be let inside their house through smart pet doors. Artificial intelligence (AI) might one day control these doors using facial recognition. That means the AI would see if the animal at the door is one it recognizes. If the AI recognizes it as an animal that lives there, the doggy door will open. This is similar to how some people's smartphones recognize their face and unlock when they hold their phone near their face.

Deep Dive

FriendChip

In 2017, a group of middle schoolers on the St. Peter's Brickbusters team from Wisconsin participated in the FIRST LEGO League world competition. This event challenges students to use science, technology, engineering, and math to solve real-world problems. The St. Peter's Brickbusters decided to focus on dogs, and they came up with the FriendChip. Since dogs are unable to tell their owners when something is wrong, their solution was a microchip that lets dog owners track their pets' blood pressure and heart rate.

Owners can also check in with their pets using phones and tablets.

Say Cheese

Ever wonder what a pet is doing when no one is around? Web cameras might be the answer. The Petcube Bites 2 Lite is a type of remote-controlled machine that lets owners watch over their pets. By using their phone, they can keep in touch with their furry friends. Owners can see, talk, listen to their pets, and even direct a machine to toss a treat to them.

A Forever Friend

Pets can be a person's best friend, but they are also a lot of work. As AI and pet technology keep improving, taking care of pets will become easier.

Taking care of pets can be hard but rewarding.

Save the Day

Wouldn't it be great to know what a pet wants or needs? Your dog might be telling you how much it enjoys going for a walk. Maybe your cat is asking for attention. Or maybe they don't feel well and need to go to the vet. AI and machine learning are working to make it happen. Communication is complicated. But someday people might really be able to understand their pets. How would you use technology to help?

Glossary

app: an application designed for a mobile device, such as a phone

artificial intelligence (AI): a computer system that is capable of imitating human intelligence

automatic: devices that operate without the help of a person

Bluetooth: a short-range wireless technology that allows users to exchange data through mobile devices

fitness: the state of being healthy

GPS: a system that uses satellite signals to navigate or find a location

microchip: a tiny piece of material containing electronic circuits that allows storage of information

pet tech: devices and technology used to take care of pets

radio-frequency identification (RFID): technology that uses radio waves to identify people or objects

veterinarian: a person who is qualified to treat the diseases and injuries of animals

Learn More

American Kennel Club: "How Do Pet Microchips Work and Should My Dog Have One?"
https://www.akc.org/expert-advice/lifestyle/how-do-dog-microchips-work/

Humane Society of the United States: "High Tech: Identifying Lost Pets with Microchips"
https://www.humanesociety.org/resources/high-tech-identifying-lost-pets-microchips

Moore, Arden. *A Kid's Guide to Dogs*. North Adams, MA: Storey, 2020.

Nugent, Samantha, and Jared Siemens. *Cat*. New York: AV2, 2022.

St. George's University: "Taking Care of Animals: Pro Tips for Pet Owners"
https://www.sgu.edu/blog/veterinary/tips-on-taking-care-of-animals/

Walker, Tracy Sue. *Bionic Animals*. Minneapolis: Lerner Publications, 2024.

Index

Photo Acknowledgments

Image credits: LuckyBusiness/iStock/Getty Images, p. 5; T3 Magazine/Future/Getty Images, p. 6; alexei_tm/iStock/Getty Images, p. 7; invisible invisible/Shutterstock, p. 9; Vershinin89/Shutterstock, p. 10; muslody.com/Shutterstock, p. 11; Lightspruch/iStock/Getty Images, p. 12; cmannphoto/E+/Getty Images, p. 13; Vera Duchovskaja/iStock/Getty Images, p. 14; Oreolife/Alamy, p. 15; LightField Studios/Shutterstock, p. 17; Sergey Mironov/Moment/Getty Images, p. 19; Eudyptula/Shutterstock, p. 20; Stefanie Keenan/Getty Images Entertainment/Getty Images, p. 21; Gregory Sweeney/Moment/Getty Images, p. 23; Purple Collar Pet Photography/Moment/Getty Images, p. 24; loocmill/Shutterstock, p. 25; whyframestudio/iStock/Getty Images, p. 27; BJI/Blue Jean Images/Getty Images, p. 28.

Cover: Nils Jacobi/Shutterstock.